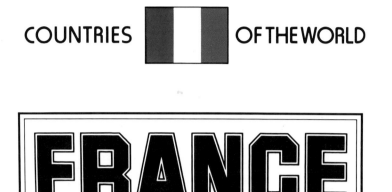

COUNTRIES OF THE WORLD

FRANCE

Alan Blackwood and Brigitte Chosson

with photographs by Chris Fairclough

Illustrated by Stefan Chabluk

The Bookwright Press
New York · 1988

Titles in this series

France   New Zealand

Great Britain   West Germany

Cover *The grape harvest in the Beaujolais region.*

Opposite *The Eiffel Tower in Paris.*

First published in the
United States in 1988 by
The Bookwright Press
387 Park Avenue South
New York, NY 10016

First published in 1988 by
Wayland (Publishers) Ltd
61 Western Road, Hove
East Sussex BN3 1JD, England

© Copyright 1988 Wayland (Publishers) Ltd

Library of Congress Cataloging-in-Publication Data
Blackwood, Alan, 1929-
    France.

    Bibliography: p.
    Includes index.
    1. France — Civilization — Juvenile literature.
I. Title.
DC33.B53   1988   944   87-33859
ISBN 0-531-18186-3

Typeset by Oliver Dawkins Ltd.,
Burgess Hill, West Sussex
Printed in Italy by G. Canale and C.S.p.A., Turin

Contents

All words that appear in **bold** are explained in the glossary on page 46.

1 Introducing France

Population: 54,335,000 (1982 census)

Capital city: Paris (population 2,188,918)

Main cities: Lyons, Marseille, Bordeaux, Toulouse, Nantes, Nice

Overseas Departments: St. Pierre and Miquelon, Guadeloupe, Martinique, French Guiana, Réunion, Crozet

Overseas Territories: Wallis and Futuna, French Polynesia, New Caledonia.

Overseas Departments are part of France while Territories have more independence.

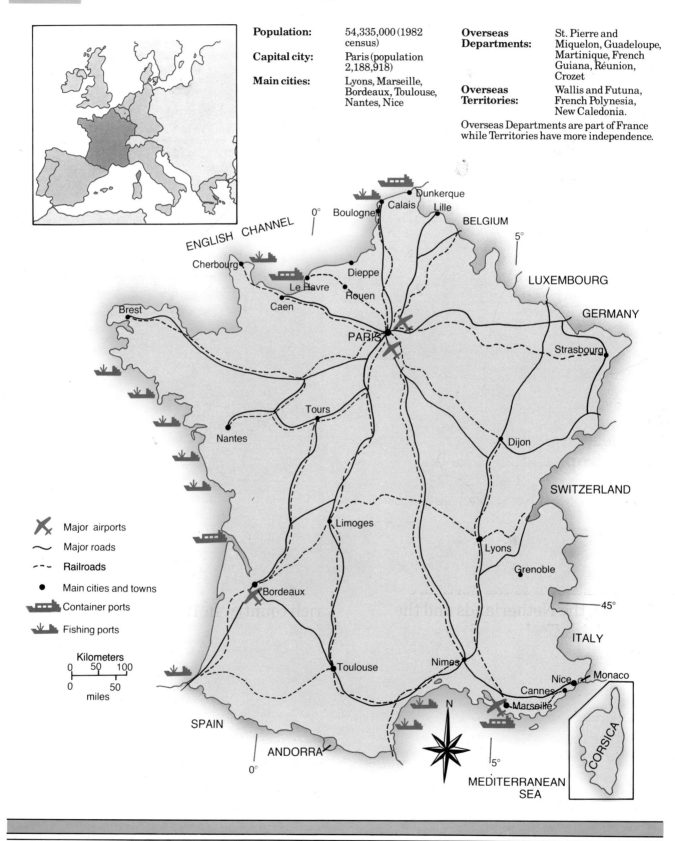

Legend:
- ✈ Major airports
- ⌒ Major roads
- - - - Railroads
- ● Main cities and towns
- 🚢 Container ports
- 🚢 Fishing ports

Kilometers
0 50 100

0 50
miles

A view of Paris from the top of the Eiffel Tower.

France is the largest country in western Europe, with an area of 547,026 sq km (211,206 sq mi). It is almost square in shape, roughly 800 km (497 mi) in each direction. France is divided into twenty-two **Metropolitan regions,** one of which is the island of Corsica off the coast of Italy. France also has a number of overseas possessions in other parts of the world.

France stands right in the middle of western Europe. To the north are Belgium, the Netherlands and the British Isles. To the south are Spain and Portugal. From west to east, it stretches all the way from the Atlantic Ocean to the Rhine River and the borders of Germany, Switzerland and Italy.

France is famous for many things: its great artists and buildings; its marvelous foods and wines; its fashions; its beautiful scenery. Today it is also a

Azay-le-Rideau is a beautiful château.

rich country. In 1957 France became a founder member of the **European Economic Community (EEC).** This created a much bigger market for its agriculture and industry, and greatly increased production. As a result, France now has one of the highest standards of living in the world. Membership in the EEC has also given France an important new role to play in world affairs.

2 Land and climate

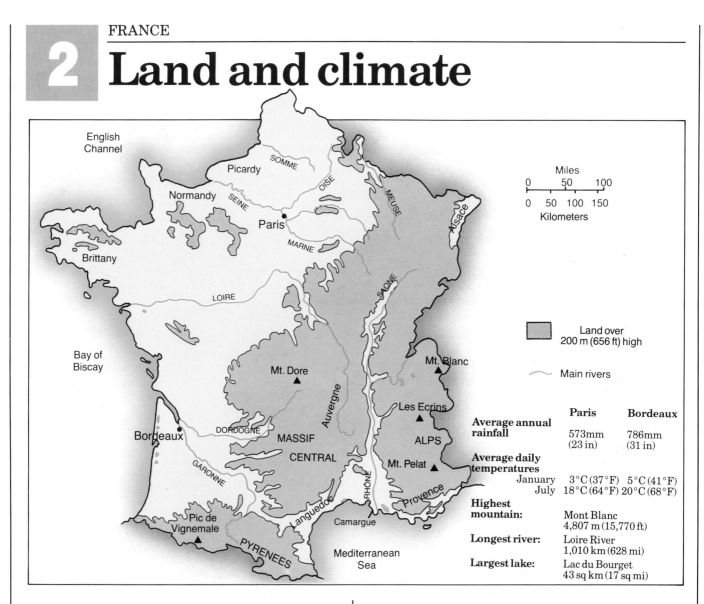

English Channel

SOMME

Picardy

OISE

Normandy

SEINE

MEUSE

Paris

Alsace

MARNE

Brittany

SAÔNE

LOIRE

Bay of Biscay

Mt. Dore ▲

Mt. Blanc ▲

Auvergne

Les Ecrins ▲

Bordeaux

DORDOGNE

MASSIF

ALPS

CENTRAL

Mt. Pelat ▲

GARONNE

RHÔNE

Provence

Pic de Vignemale ▲

Languedoc

Camargue

PYRENEES

Mediterranean Sea

Miles
0   50   100

0   50 100 150
Kilometers

Land over 200 m (656 ft) high

Main rivers

	Paris	Bordeaux
Average annual rainfall	573mm (23 in)	786mm (31 in)
Average daily temperatures		
January	3°C (37°F)	5°C (41°F)
July	18°C (64°F)	20°C (68°F)
Highest mountain:	Mont Blanc 4,807 m (15,770 ft)	
Longest river:	Loire River 1,010 km (628 mi)	
Largest lake:	Lac du Bourget 43 sq km (17 sq mi)	

France is a land of contrasts in both scenery and climate. It is bounded by seas and mountains and crossed by many rivers. In general, France has a **temperate** climate but there are regional variations. Nearly the whole country has from 500 to 1,270 mm (20–50 in) of rain annually. The north, west and southwest generally have cool summers and mild winters with rain mainly in the autumn. The climate of the Massif Central and eastern France is more continental, with cold winters and warm summers. The south coast, on the Mediterranean Sea, has hot, dry summers and warm winters with occasional rain. A well-known local feature is the *mistral*, a cold, dry wind most common in winter, blowing strongly from the north down the Rhône valley.

Facing the English Channel in the north are the chalky cliffs, plains and pastures of Picardy and Normandy. Farther west, the rocky coasts of Brittany face the stormy Atlantic Ocean, while hundreds of miles of sandy beaches and pine forests mark the edge of the Bay of Biscay.

Much of inland France is meadow and woodland, all the way from the Ile-de-France (the Paris region) and the valley of the Loire River to the Dordogne River farther south. But in the center there is the large area of the Massif Central. This is wild highland country, dominated by a region of ancient extinct volcanoes in the Auvergne. North and eastward again are the rolling, wooded hills of Burgundy, Alsace and the Jura, near Switzerland.

France has the highest mountain in Europe — Mont Blanc 4,807 m (15,770 ft) in the Alps. The Pyrenees, to the south, are another mighty mountain range. Between these mountains lie the regions of Provence and Languedoc, lapped by the warm Mediterranean Sea, where cypress and olive trees, lavender and sweet-smelling herbs flourish in the long, hot summers. Along the south coast stretches the glamorous French Riviera.

Corsica, the mountainous and rocky-coasted island in the Mediterranean Sea, is famous for its rugged scenery and fragrant **maquis** vegetation.

A beautiful field of lavender in the Alps. Fragrant plant oils are used in France's world-famous perfume industry.

Below *The coast on the Côte d'Azur.*

Left *The spectacular Pont d'Arc across the Ardèche River, which flows into the Rhône.*

3 Wildlife

Wild boar in a forest glade.

The wide-open spaces of France, and the many changes of scenery, provide a varied **habitat** for an abundance of wildlife. Foxes, badgers, rabbits and hares, larks, blackbirds, woodpeckers, magpies and owls, grass snakes and adders, are found almost everywhere in France, as in other European countries. And in summer, **migratory** swifts, swallows and martins make their home in every town and village. The lovely song of the nightingale can be heard during the early summer months.

In certain areas there are some more unusual creatures. In the Auvergne (a mainly mountainous region), there are wild boar (ancestors of farmyard pigs), large, fierce animals with bristly hair and tusks. During cold winters there are even reports of wolves.

Alsace is famous for its storks — large birds with long necks and beaks, that make their nests among the roofs and steeples of sleepy towns and villages. High in the Alps and the Pyrenees the chamois, or mountain goat, may be seen, and occasionally an eagle. Both are rare and protected species.

Above A white stork with its nest, perched on a rooftop.

Below A herd of chamoix, a mountain goat that lives in the Alps.

In Provence there are brightly colored summer butterflies and moths, lizards, cicadas, large green grasshoppers and small brown scorpions. By rivers and streams the bull frogs croak loudly at night.

On the edge of Provence, where the Rhône River flows into the Mediterranean Sea, is the flat, marshy area called the Camargue, famous for its great flocks of pink flamingos and herds of white horses.

Below Some of the famous flamingos of the Carmargue.

4 The colorful past

Because of its geographical position in Europe, France has had one of the most eventful histories of any European nation. The Romans first conquered the land around 50 B.C. and named it Gaul. Then it was attacked by the Huns, Goths and Saxons from the east, the Moors of Spain from the south, and the Vikings from the north. Around A.D. 800, a Germanic tribe called the Franks, led by King Charlemagne, invaded France and built up a great empire that included much of present-day Germany and Italy.

In the **Middle Ages,** rivalry with England began. English kings claimed large parts of France. But in the fifteenth century the French heroine, Joan of Arc, rallied the French armies and finally the English were driven out.

France and England kept on quarreling, with more wars in Europe, and in parts of their rival overseas empires, such as India and Canada. Between 1789 and 1793, there was a revolution in France that began with the storming of the Bastille prison in Paris (now celebrated each July 14 with a national holiday). The Revolution ended with the forming of a **republic.** At about this time Napoleon rose to power and led the French armies. Napoleon successfully invaded other European countries but Britain joined with other nations to defeat him.

Important dates

A.D. 486	Clovis defeats the Romans near Soissons and founds a new Frankish kingdom, the beginning of France.	1870	Third Republic declared after defeat of Napoleon III by the Prussian army. The true beginning of republican France.
768	Charlemagne crowned king of the Franks; afterward he creates the Holy Roman Empire.	1914–18	World War I.
		1939–45	World War II.
1226	Louis IX crowned king, the greatest medieval French monarch.	1946	Foundation of the Fourth Republic, after liberation by the Allies.
1431	Joan of Arc burned at the stake during the Hundred Years' War with England. Joan had defeated the English and reestablished the French crown.	1958	France joins the EEC. Charles De Gaulle elected president. Beginning of the Fifth Republic.
		1969	Georges Pompidou succeeds as president after De Gaulle's resignation.
1643	Louis XIV crowned king. Known as "The Sun King," he made France the strongest European power.	1974	Death of Pompidou. Valéry Giscard d'Estaing becomes president.
1789	Storming of the Bastille prison in Paris and start of the Revolution, leading to the rule of Napoleon and the Napoleonic Wars.	1981	François Mitterand elected president.

Above *A painting by the French artist David, of the coronation of Napoleon in 1804.*

Right *General de Gaulle on a visit to Algeria. He became president of France and established the Fifth Republic.*

In the nineteenth century, France's new rival and enemy was Germany. In World War I (1914–18), France and Britain were **allies** against the German Empire. Much of the fighting took place in France, and over a million French soldiers were killed before victory was gained.

In World War II (1939–45), France was defeated and occupied by Nazi Germany. After **liberation** by the Allies (Britain and the United States), the French economy began to recover. France then had to fight bitter wars in two of its **colonies** (Vietnam and Algeria), which were fighting for independence. But under the leadership of President de Gaulle, France gave up its colonies. He was determined to make France strong and prosperous again.

5 The French people

Left A typical café, where people love to sit and talk while they drink beer, wine or coffee.

Below Young French people of many different ethnic groups.

The French people are a mixture of many races: Celts, Latins, Normans, Vikings, Franks and Saxons.

The population is about the same as that of Britain — nearly 56 million people — despite the fact that France is more than twice the size of Britain. There are several reasons why the population is not greater. France remained a largely agricultural land, with most people still living in the country, when other nations had big new industrial cities crowded with people. Also, France lost so many soldiers during the Napoleonic wars (1799–1815) and then during World War I that for a time the population actually decreased.

Since World War II things have changed completely. The population has grown rapidly. At the same time, people have moved away from the farms and villages and into the towns and cities, where they can earn more money in industry and commerce. People from the old French colonies, especially Algeria, have also moved to the cities of France.

Today, over 10 million people live and work in the Paris region, which is the most prosperous part of the country. This means that about one in every six French people now live in or near the capital. Lyons, Marseilles, and the industrial area around Lille, also have populations of over a million people each.

The French still take pride in the traditional ways of life of the provinces. In Brittany and Alsace, Provence, or the Basque region on the borders of Spain, they have their own special costumes, songs and dances, arts and crafts.

Children dressed in the traditional costumes of the Alsace region of eastern France.

6 Paris

This is the cathedral of Notre Dame overlooking the Seine River.

Paris has drawn people to it like a magnet ever since it became the nation's capital nearly a thousand years ago. Rich or ambitious people, wanting to get on in the world, and many more simply looking for work, have been attracted to Paris from every corner of France. The French themselves call it "The City of Light" — the place where everything is always going on.

This is why Paris has had such a large population for so long. People have always wanted to live close to the center, so they prefer to live in apartments rather than in a house with a yard farther out of town. The *concierge*, or caretaker, with a small office by the main entrance to almost every block of apartments, has a special place in French town and city life.

Even today, with more and more people living in the Paris region rather than in the crowded city itself, there are few of the sprawling **suburbs** that are found around many European cities. Instead, there are new **satellite towns,** with apartments, stores, arts and recreation centers all in one small area.

Meanwhile, the historic center of Paris is being renewed. There is the gleaming new Centre Beaubourg or Pompidou Center (named after President Georges Pompidou who started it), built on the site of an old Paris market. More recently, an abandoned railroad station, the Gare d'Orsay, has been turned into a magnificent new art gallery. What is happening in Paris is also happening in Lyons, Marseilles, Lille, Bordeaux, Rouen, Toulouse, and the other big towns and cities of the provinces.

Above Modern apartment blocks at Evry, one of the "satellite towns" near Paris.

Below The fountains outside the Pompidou Center, Paris, with strange and comic sculptures.

7 Growing up in the city

Few children growing up in a big town or city live in a house with a yard. But apartments are often quite large, with two or three bedrooms, a big living room, kitchen and bathroom.

Normal working days, including school days, start early and finish late, although the French make up for this with long vacations. Breakfast will probably be a bit hurried, with little time for anything more than a bowl of cereal, a *tartine* (bread and jam) or a *croissant* (flaky roll) and *café au lait* (coffee with milk).

The children may have lunch at school, or go home if it's not too far to travel. They will have a snack when they come home from school.

A quick family breakfast at the start of the day.

Above A young schoolgirl does her homework in a corner of her bedroom.

For many families, *dîner,* the main meal, is in the evening, when everybody is together again. They often sit down to soup, ham and other cold meats, a hot meat or fish dish with vegetables, and a fresh green salad, followed finally by cheese and fruit. Most French families, including the children, also drink wine at mealtimes.

When the children have done their homework many like to watch television (quiz shows and cartoons are favorite programs) or read the comic strips in newspapers and books. Visits to the movies are popular too, and teenagers like to meet at the local café (coffeehouse).

Today, many large towns and cities also have a *Maison des Jeunes* (Youth Center), well-equipped recreation centers, with sports facilities, electronic games and a library.

When the children have finished their homework, this family likes to relax together watching television.

8 Life in the country

Many country children form part of a larger family circle than those in towns and cities. This is because it is much more usual in the country for grandparents, parents and children to live in a fairly large house, rather than in a city apartment.

Thirty years ago there were big differences between town and country life in France. In some villages you could still see people walking around in wooden clogs, collecting water from a pump, or driving a horse and cart. Such rustic sights are very rare today. Now that most people have a car for shopping in the nearest town, and everybody watches the same television programs, the traditional ways of country life are disappearing fast.

Above A boy helps his father dig potatoes.

Above top A farmer with his ox cart, a rare sight today.

However, some differences do remain. Children living on a farm often get up earlier than city children, to lend a hand feeding the poultry or putting the cattle out to pasture. At harvest time they often work in the fields after they have come home from school. They may also have quite a long journey to and from school, by bike or on a special school bus. All this gives them less free time than city boys and girls.

In France there is a great tradition of Sunday lunch. Townspeople like to make up a party and go to a restaurant, but country families usually prepare a big meal at home, for family and friends. Starting with an *apéritif* (a drink taken before a meal), Sunday lunch in the country can last all afternoon.

Sunday lunch in an Ardèche farmhouse with family and friends.

9 Education

The majority of French children receive free education in state schools, though there are private schools run by the Roman Catholic Church and other institutions.

The stages of French schooling are carefully and precisely planned, like the rungs of a ladder. French boys and girls start to climb the ladder at three or four years old with the play school, or *maternelle.* Elementary school lasts for five years and is followed by four years at a general high school. Some go to trade schools where they receive job training.

Left *Village children, proud to be photographed with their teacher.*

Below *Hard at work in a village school.*

Right Relaxing after school.

Below Time off from classes is enjoyed in the playground.

French children go to school on Saturday mornings, but they all have Wednesdays free. School hours, generally from 8:30 a.m. to 5:30 p.m., are longer than in most other countries, and during their years at secondary school, French schoolchildren also get plenty of homework. But they still find time to relax. There are two hours off for lunch, and plenty of opportunities for hobbies and sports.

At the age of sixteen, high school pupils take the BEPC *(Brevet Elementaire Premier Cycle)* examination. The age for leaving school is sixteen, but with all that hard work behind them, many French teenagers think it worthwhile to stay on for another year or two, to take the exam *"Le Bac" (Le Baccalauréat)*. For many French teenagers it is the climax to their school career. If they pass, they can go straight on to a university.

10 Shopping

Every French town has its market day. In some towns there are special buildings that house the market under one big glass roof. In others, there is a market square, filled with colorful stalls. Farmers come from the surrounding countryside to sell their own produce, such as fruit, flowers, vegetables or eggs. Besides food stalls there may be others selling clothes, tools and all sorts of household goods.

Everybody loves the bustle of market day. But today many people shop in a *hypermarché* (hypermarket). The French also call them *"les grandes surfaces"* (the big areas). They are surrounded by huge parking lots, and inside you can find

Above *Fresh vegetables on sale at an open-air market. The French people like buying fresh produce daily rather than shopping weekly.*

Below *French money and stamps. The franc is divided into 100 centimes.*

everything from deep-frozen lobsters to lawnmowers. The *hypermarchés* at Calais, Boulogne and Dunkirk are very popular with the British because it is easy for them to catch a ferry across the English Channel on a day trip.

Many French people still prefer the small specialty shops. The *boulangerie* is a baker's shop, where long, crunchy white loaves *(baguettes)* and croissants are sold. The French like their bread to be fresh and often go to the baker's twice a day. There are also *patisseries* that specialize in pastries, cakes, chocolates and sweets. The *boucherie* is an ordinary butcher's shop. A *charcuterie* at one time specialized in pork products, including tasty, spiced pork sausages, but today, many *charcuteries* are more like delicatessens.

Two other types of shops to look for are the *pharmacie* (chemist), and *maison de la presse* for newspapers, magazines and books.

Above *France is famous for its large variety of cheeses. This splendid display is in a store in Vichy.*

Left *A fish store in the heart of Paris.*

11 Sports and leisure

Le Sport is big business in France, and *L'Equipe (The Team)* is one of the country's best-selling newspapers.

Auto racing first started in France and two of the sport's biggest events still take place there. The Le Mans 24-hour race lasts all one day and night, and the winners are the team whose car travels the greatest distance in the time. The Monaco Grand Prix is a race through the steep, winding streets of Monte Carlo, in the small **principality** of Monaco on the French Riviera. This dangerous car race attracts many visitors.

The Monaco Grand Prix is a race through the streets of Monte Carlo.

Competitors in the grueling Tour de France *hurtling across the* Place de la Concorde, *Paris.*

Bicycle racing is another favorite sport. The climax of the cycling season is the annual *Tour de France,* a difficult and tiring race that is organized in stages and lasts several weeks. Cyclists come from many countries to compete. The race covers 4,023 km (2,500 mi), up and down mountains, during the hottest time of the year.

Among spectator sports the most popular are two types of football — rugby and soccer. France has won the International Rugby Football Championship many times. But *Le Foot* to French fans means soccer. Big clubs, like Paris St. Germain and St. Etienne, regularly win a place in European competitions. The national team is strong as well. They have been European champions, and also reached the semi-final of the World Cup in Mexico in 1986.

Nothing is more typically French than the old game of *boule,* something like lawn bowling, but using metal balls, which the players toss into the air instead of rolling along the ground. Many towns and villages, especially in The Midi (The South) have a "boule park" — an area of ground marked out under shady trees — where local competitions attract much interest and excitement.

Fishing is a very popular pastime in France, thanks to the country's thousands of streams, rivers and lakes. There are many huntsmen too, out with their guns, once the hunting season has begun.

These traditional pastimes are only a tiny part of the activities that French people enjoy today. Hot air ballooning was started in France (back in 1783), and some companies run ballooning trips. There are also wind-surfing, canoeing and yachting. And in winter, trains take skiing enthusiasts to resorts in the Alps, Pyrenees, and the mountains of the Auvergne and Cevennes. The Winter Olympics have been held at Grenoble in southeastern France. Schools also organize skiing trips during the winter vacations.

A game of boule, *a favorite pastime in many parts of France.*

The summer vacation season begins at the end of July, when the whole nation suddenly seems to be on the move, and the main roads out of Paris and other big cities are packed with cars and trailers. *Le Camping* is extremely popular. There are well-run campsites all over the country, with facilities like washrooms and toilets provided, where you can rent a space for your camper or tent. Many French families reserve the same space for their summer vacation each year.

Even on picnics the French like to do things in style. Folding tables and chairs are the secret for keeping the ants away from the food!

Above *There are many books and magazines for this girl to choose from.*

Above top *Fishing in a lake at Chantilly, near Paris.*

12 Religion

A tragic episode in French history: the massacre of French Huguenots at Cahors in 1561.

The main religion of France is Roman Catholicism, but France has had quite a stormy religious history.

In the Middle Ages, a religious group in southern France, called the Cathars (meaning Purists), was destroyed in a savage war known as the Albigensian Crusade (named after the town of Albi).

Then, at the time of the **Reformation** during the sixteenth century, many French people became Protestants called Huguenots, and there was more bloodshed and hatred between them and the Roman Catholics.

Finally, during the French Revolution (1789–93), the Church itself was attacked; and from that time on, the functions of Church and State have been kept separate.

All this has affected religion and the place of the Church in France today. French couples have two wedding ceremonies. It is the law that they must be married in their local town hall. Then their families usually want them to have a church wedding as well. Opposite you can see a wedding feast after both ceremonies.

In other ways, religious life has survived all the upsets of the past. Most families still observe the Catholic *Profession de Foi* (Profession of Faith), when boys and girls of eleven or twelve years of age take **Communion** and receive **Confirmation.** Children also like to celebrate their Name Day, which is the day of the year commemorating the saint from whom they take their own Christian name. It is rather like having a second birthday.

All the important Church festivals also live on. Christmas, Easter, Ascension Day (in May) and Pentecost (in May or June) are all celebrated with public holidays.

One of the most famous Roman Catholic shrines is in France, at Lourdes, near the Pyrenees. A peasant girl named Bernadette claimed to have seen the Virgin Mary there; now people from around the world make annual pilgrimages to the site, many hoping to be cured of some sickness or disease.

Pilgrims visiting the famous Roman Catholic shrine at Lourdes.

A wedding celebration in Brittany.

13 Artistic France

Everywhere you go in France, there are reminders of a glorious artistic past. There are beautiful churches and cathedrals built in the Romanesque (Norman) and Gothic styles, which inspired, in their turn, many of the great English cathedrals. There are all the famous **châteaux,** looking like fairy-tale castles. Most magnificent of all is the Palace of Versailles, near Paris, with gardens, lakes, fountains and woods that stretch for many miles.

Left *The great Gothic cathedral at Amiens.*

Below Luncheon of the Boating Party *by the French Impressionist artist Renoir.*

Just as famous are the group of French painters known as the Impressionists, notably Edouard Manet, Auguste Renoir and Claude Monet. They revolutionized the art world in the nineteenth century, with their paintings showing the effects of light and shade, sunshine and rain. The artist Pablo Picasso was born in Spain in 1881, but spent most of his life in France, and with other French artists he created Cubism and other movements in modern art.

The French sometimes stage *son et lumière* performances at famous buildings or historic sites. This is the use of floodlighting, words and music to re-live colorful events of the past associated with historic buildings.

Paris has been the home of many famous writers and playwrights (Molière, Voltaire, Victor Hugo) and composers (Hector Berlioz, Claude Debussy, Maurice Ravel). It has many theaters and a splendid Opera House.

The French have also been pioneers in motion pictures. The Lumière Brothers produced the first practical motion-picture camera and projector, and opened the world's first movie house in Paris in 1895. Ever since, France has been making films by such world-famous directors as Jean Renoir (son of the Impressionist painter) and François Truffaut. And the Cannes film festival on the Riviera attracts movie stars and directors from all over the world.

Above right The Sleeping Beauty *ballet being performed at* l'Opéra *in Paris.*

Right *Louis Lumière with an early film projector.*

14 Fashion and design

When the French say somebody or something is *"à la mode,"* they are speaking of fashion. France has always been a leader in elegant and fashionable living. The clothes of Louis XIV's court at Versailles in the seventeenth century were copied all over the Western world.

Haute Couture is the name for high-quality dressmaking and design. Each spring and autumn the big Paris fashion houses (Yves St. Laurent, Christian Dior, Coco Chanel and others) hold exhibitions of their latest "creations." Within a few days these will appear in every fashion magazine, at home and abroad.
The clothes will be on sale in Paris itself, and in London, New York and other cities around the world where rich and fashion-conscious people live. Soon they will influence the look of the clothes we all wear.

This taste for elegant living has taken many other forms down the centuries. In the Middle Ages, there were beautiful tapestries to decorate the stone walls of castles and mansions. The towns of Gobelin and Aubusson are associated with some of the finest tapestries.

Sèvres, another small town, not far from Paris, owes its fame to the lovely delicate porcelain bowls and jars, cups, saucers and small statues that its craftsmen made in the eighteenth century. At this time other French craftsmen were making beautiful and ornate clocks and furniture.

Above *A model at a fashion show.*

There is nothing to compare with French perfume. This ancient industry is traditionally based on the lavender and other flowers of southern France. The center of the French perfume industry is found in the small town of Grasse, near Cannes. It is one of France's major growth industries. Perfumes made by such famous firms as Chanel, Carven, Guy Laroche and Lanvin, are an essential part of living *"à la mode"*

Above *A magnificent Gobelin tapestry.*

Left *Blue Sèvres porcelain dating from the eighteenth century.*

15 Farming, fishing and food

France has more fertile agricultural land than any other country in Europe. And the different soils and changing weather conditions from north to south and from west to east allow farmers across the country to produce a marvelous variety of crops.

Normandy, with its rich pastures, is the region of dairy farming. The chalky plains of the Ile-de-France are ideal for growing wheat, barley and corn. Up in the hills of Burgundy, and along the banks of the Saône River in east France, the farmers breed white Charollais cattle for beef. The Auvergne has excellent grazing for sheep and goats. From Provence and Languedoc come delicious cherries, strawberries, peaches, melons, tomatoes and olives.

There are plenty of seafoods: flounder, sole and turbot from the English Channel; shellfish from Brittany; sardines from the Mediterranean.

France is well known as the land of *haute cuisine* (high-class cooking), and every region has its specialties.

Above White Charollais cattle are raised for beef.

Below Mouthwatering cherries from the Rhône Valley.

Normandy's cooking is based on its cream and butter, its cider and the apple brandy called calvados.

Burgundy is famous for its *escargots*, which are large edible snails, served piping hot with garlic butter. The streams of the Auvergne and neighboring Perigord are the places for delicious freshwater fish dishes, of trout, pike and crayfish. This part of France is also famous for truffles, a kind of mushroom that grows under the ground and is highly prized for its flavor.

In the town of Montelimar in the Rhône valley, they make *nougat*, the mouthwatering white fudge made from local honey and almonds. To the south, in Provence, a specialty is glacé fruits, preserved in sugar. A quite different local dish is the famous *bouillabaisse* fish soup. And nearly every region of France produces its own special kind of cheese.

Above Hunting for truffles with a pig. The farmer is holding a truffle in his hand.

16 A land of wine

Vineyards and villages of the Alsace wine region.

For most French people, wine is a vital part of good living and France produces some of the very best wine in the world. Wine is made from fermented grape juice, in which sugar in the juice has been changed into alcohol. The grapes are grown in specially cultivated vineyards. Most regions of France have vineyards and produce their own wine. The wines of each region have their own special flavor. Many factors contribute to this: the type of vine that is grown; the condition of the soil; whether the land is flat or hilly; and how much rain and sunshine there is.

The vineyards around Bordeaux

produce strong red wines, thanks to all the hot summer sun. Farther north, along the banks of the Loire River, and in Alsace, they make lighter white wines. The region of Burgundy, half way between the warm south and the cooler north, is famous for both excellent red and white wines.

Another type of wine that France is famous for is Champagne. This is made by putting the wine in bottles and corking it up while it is still fermenting. It is this process that makes it fizz with bubbles and sparkle in the glass.

Cognac and Armagnac are the names of two French brandies, which are made from white wine. The brandy is stored in oak casks or barrels for several years before being bottled, which gives it its special flavor and "bouquet" or aroma.

Above Bunches of grapes almost ready for the harvest.

Right Tending the vines.

17 Industry

Above Concorde *climbing away from the Charles de Gaulle Airport, Paris. It was built jointly by French and British engineers.*

Below *This is a Renault factory. France's auto industry is one of the largest in the world.*

France lagged behind Britain, Germany and the United States in the **Industrial Revolution** because it was short of coal. However, it has made up for this with an industrial revolution of its own since World War II.

The government has built many hydro-electric generating stations, harnessing the power of large rivers, like the swift-flowing Rhône River, and waterfalls in the mountainous regions of the Alps and the Pyrenees. More recently it has added to this program with nuclear power stations. French engineers have also built a tidal power station in the Rance estuary, the first of its kind in the world. All this cheap electricity has encouraged the expansion of existing industries and promoted the growth of new ones in all parts of France.

French scientists have also been experimenting with solar power. This abundance of energy, plus important new mining operations (iron ore in Lorraine, uranium in the Massif Central), have helped to turn France into today's industrial giant.

Iron and steel, shipbuilding, building railroad cars and locomotives, electronics, textiles, cement (thanks to all the chalk and limestone) and **pharmaceuticals**, all play a big part in the industrial scene.

The aircraft and auto industries are found mainly in the Paris area. France's auto industry is one of the world's biggest. Renault, Citroen and Peugeot-

| Main exports: | Iron and steel, machinery, motor vehicles, textiles, wine, fruit and vegetables |
| Main imports: | Crude oil, minerals, chemicals |

Above The cooling towers of the nuclear power station at Cruas on the Rhône River.

Talbot lead the way in the manufacture of cars, trucks and buses. The company called Michelin is equally famous for the production of rubber tires.

Aérospatiale and Dassault are world famous for aircraft design and production. Aérospatiale at Toulouse, in cooperation with the British Rolls-Royce company, built the world's first supersonic passenger jet, *Concorde.*

There is, also, the petrochemical industry. France has lacked oil of its own, just as it has lacked coal. But it imports large quantities of crude oil, mainly from North Africa, and has huge refineries around Marseilles, Lyons and along the Seine River, close to other centers of industry.

Other industries include electrical engineering, leather, ceramics, jewelry, watchmaking, the famous perfume industry and the tourist industry.

18 Transportation

Paris is the heart of France, so all transportation systems focus on it. Because it is a big city Paris needs its own transportation networks. The Paris Métro was one of the world's first subway systems. In recent years it has been modernized, with new express lines and trains that run on rubber tires for greater speed and comfort. Lyons and Marseilles have also built Métro lines.

The state-owned railroads, called SNCF *(Société Nationale des Chemins de Fer Français),* are as fast and efficient as any in the world. They include 11,000 km (6,800 mi) of electrified line. The pride of the system is the fleet of high-speed trains called TGVs (*Trains Grande Vitesse*) that run between Paris and other big cities at speeds of up to 290 kph (180 mph).

Above A train in the Paris Métro.

Above *The Paris* Boulevard Périphérique *at night.*

Above Aircraft at Charles de Gaulle Airport.

Right A more relaxed way to travel: a motor launch cruises along a Burgundy canal.

The principal French highways (*autoroutes*) are linked to a multilane highway, the *Boulevard Périphérique*, that runs around central Paris. Drivers have to pay a toll to drive on the *autoroutes* (outside the big cities), which can be quite expensive over a long distance. Other main roads, the *routes nationales*, are free.

France is a large and wealthy country so it has an important international airline. Air France has one of the world's largest fleets of aircraft. This includes the supersonic airliner, *Concorde*, which flies regularly between Paris and New York, a distance of 5,792 km (3,600 mi), in well under four hours.

But not everything in France goes with a rush. The government has taken care of the country's canals. Besides being used extensively as a cheap way of transporting goods, they are a big tourist attraction. By river and canal it is possible to go by boat all the way from the English Channel to the Mediterranean, with plenty of time to relax and enjoy the countryside.

19 Government

In 1793, during the Revolution, the French people executed King Louis XVI and Queen Marie Antoinette. Although there were later attempts to restore the **monarchy**, France has been a republic for most of its recent history.

A republic is a nation that has an elected president as Head of State. The French people also elect deputies to a National Assembly (a parliament) — 555 from Metropolitan France, plus a small number from former overseas colonies now politically linked with France. The government, headed by a prime minister, is formed from the political party with the majority of deputies, or from a **coalition** of parties.

Until recently, much of the government and law of France was administered through the ninety-six departments, most of which were created during the Revolution. At the same time, it is still largely based on the principles of the *Code Napoléon,* the system of administration drawn up by Napoleon I, who wished to keep most of the power in the hands of the central government. Today, the departments are grouped into twenty-two larger Metropolitan regions, which have much more governing power of their own.

A good example of logical French thinking is the way each department has a code number, which is applied

The execution of Queen Marie Antoinette in 1793, the start of republican government in France.

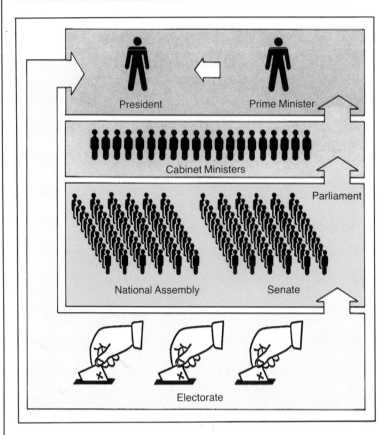

President

Prime Minister

Cabinet Ministers

Parliament

National Assembly   Senate

Electorate

The French government:
France is a democratic republic.
A president, a prime minister,
and a parliament form its present
government, called the Fifth
Republic. The president
appoints the prime minister and
the cabinet, which is headed by
the prime minister. France's
National Assembly (parliament)
is made up of deputies, elected
by voters.

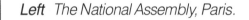

Left   The National Assembly, Paris.

Below   The last two numbers on this French registration plate tell you which department the car belongs to.

systematically to many aspects of administration. Postal codes are based on it, and so are vehicle registration numbers. The last two numbers of every French license plate are the code of the department. By looking for that, it is possible to tell which part of France every car, bus or truck comes from.

20 Facing the future

A surplus of food being stored. This is a "grain mountain."

Modern France has its problems, like every nation. There is the matter of the European Economic Community's Common Agricultural Policy (CAP), which is creating huge surpluses of food. Much of this surplus comes from France. But if the EEC and the French government decide that crop production should be cut, this will affect French farmers very badly.

France has unemployment in the old industrial coal-mining region of the northeast, and the French are also worried about the continuing movement of people from the countryside to the towns and cities. This is threatening the economy and the whole way of life of many of the rural regions.

Some French people are anxious about the French language. In times past many

French words entered other languages. Today, hundreds of English and American words and phrases (for example, *le weekend*) are used in everyday French; "Franglais" is a cross between the two languages.

But in science and technology, France is forging ahead. Its *Ariane* space rockets and electronics are an essential part of plans for European satellite television. Its micro-technology has just created a new kind of credit card, known as the *carte à la puce* or "flea card" (because the little micro-chip it holds looks much like a flea). It is almost like carrying a bank around in your pocket.

France has a stake in the European Atomic Energy Community (Euratom) program for research into thermo-nuclear energy; and it is already using energy from the sun and the oceans.

The Frenchman Jacques Cousteau has fascinated people with his exploration of the seas and oceans. France has a new oceanic research ship that can electronically chart the ocean floor. It has also built *Nautile,* a submarine equipped with powerful lamps and television cameras, that can plunge 6,000 meters (19,685 ft) down to the very deepest parts of the ocean. In ocean-ography, France is leading the world.

Above top The Ariane *space rocket is built in Toulouse but is launched in South America from the French colony of Guiana.*

Right *The French are world leaders in oceanography. This French–American oceanographic expedition took place in 1974.*

Glossary

Allies Nations fighting on the same side in a war.

Château The French word for "castle," but also describing any large residence, once the home of a king or queen or a noble family. The plural is châteaux.

Coalition A grouping of political parties with some of the same policies or objectives, often to form a government.

Colony A territory occupied and governed by people from another country; an overseas possession.

Communion Most important service of the Roman Catholic and other religions.

Confirmation A ceremony of the Christian Church by which people become full members.

European Economic Community (EEC) The group of twelve European nations working toward economic union. France and Britain are member nations. Another name for it is the Common Market.

Habitat The natural home or environment of different animals and plants.

Industrial Revolution The rapid growth of industries, based mainly on coal and steam power, that took place in some Western countries during the late eighteenth and nineteenth centuries.

Liberation The freeing of countries from Nazi occupation by the Allies (see above) during World War II.

Maquis A French word for the thick growth of shrubs and herbs covering much of the south of France and Corsica. Also the name of the patriots who resisted Nazi occupation during World War II.

Metropolitan regions The main administrative regions of mainland France (plus the island of Corsica).

Middle Ages The long period of European history, from about A.D. 1000 to 1500.

Migratory Relating to migration, when animals, especially birds, move from one habitat to another during the seasons of the year. Such moves are often over thousands of miles.

Monarchy A nation with a king or queen as Head of State.

Pharmaceuticals Medical drugs and other medicines; from the Greek word *pharmakon*, "a drug."

Principality A country, usually quite small, with a prince or princess as Head of State.

Reformation The religious movement, of the fifteenth and sixteenth centuries, that broke away from the Roman Catholic Church and formed the Protestant Churches.

Republic A nation without a monarch, usually with an elected president as Head of State.

Satellite town A town that is, usually separated by open country from a larger town or city, but connected with it economically and socially. Often created specially to house people from the city.

Suburbs Districts surrounding the central areas of a large town or city.

Temperate A climate without extremes of heat or cold, and with adequate rainfall throughout the year.

Books to read

Children's Treasure Hunt Travel to Belgium & France by Frances Goldstein. Paper Tiger Paperbacks, 1981.

Come to France by John Holland. (Warwick Press) Franklin Watts, 1979.

The Days of the Musketeers by Pierre Miquel. Silver, 1985.

France: The Crossroads of Europe by Susan Balerdi. Dillon, 1984.

France in Pictures edited & published by the Sterling Publishing Co., 1965.

French Food and Drink by Francoise Lafargue. Franklin Watts, 1984.

Here is France by Claire Bishop. Farrar, Straus & Giroux, 1969.

Take a Trip to Belgium by Keith Lye. Franklin Watts, 1984.

Take a Trip to France by Jonathan Rutland. Franklin Watts, 1981.

The Three Musketeers (Children's Edition) by Alexandre Dumas. Putnam Publishing Group, 1959.

We Live in France by James Tomlins. Franklin Watts, 1984.

Picture acknowledgments

All photographs were taken by Chris Fairclough with the exception of the following: Air France 38; Cephas Picture Library (cover); The Bridgeman Art Library 11 (top), 30, 33 (both); Bruce Coleman Ltd 8 (K. Wothe), 9 (bottom/Gordon Langsbury, left/Udo Hirsch, top/Roger Wilmshurst), 31 (top/Nicholas Devore), 35 (bottom/Michel Viard), 45 (bottom/Jeff Simon); The Hutchison Library 38, 43; The Mansell Collection 28, 31 (bottom), 42; Telefocus 45 (top); TOPHAM 11 (below), 13, 24, 25, 29, 32, 44. Maps and diagrams by Stefan Chabluk.

Index